The
Canterbury
Tales
Illustrated Prologue

The
Canterbury
Tales

Illustrated Prologue

GEOFFREY CHAUCER

EDITED BY MICHAEL ALEXANDER
BERRY PROFESSOR OF ENGLISH LITERATURE
UNIVERSITY OF ST. ANDREWS, SCOTLAND

SCALA BOOKS

Text by Larry D. Benson (Editor), The Riverside Chaucer, Third Edition, Copyright © 1987 by Houghton Mifflin Company. Reprinted with permission.

Notes and glossary © 1996 Michael Alexander, Berry Professor of English Literature, University of St Andrews, Scotland

©1996 Scala Books

First published in 1996 by Scala Books

an imprint of Philip Wilson Publishers Ltd

143-149 Great Portland Street, London W1N 5FB

Distributed for the general book trade in the USA and Canada by

Antique Collectors' Club, Market Street Industrial Park,

Wappingers' Falls, New York, NY 12590

All rights reserved.

ISBN 1 85759 113 5

Designed and typeset by Roger Davies

Printed in Lublijana, Slovenia by TLP Printing House

PHOTOGRAPHIC ACKNOWLEDGEMENTS

Grateful acknowledgement is due to the following for supplying copyright photographic material and for permission to reproduce it.

It has not been possible to source every photograph although every effort has been made to do so.

Numerals indicate page numbers of illustrations.

Bibliothèque Nationale, Paris: 32 (bottom)

Bodleian Library, Oxford: 2, 3, 8, 10 (border), 12, 14, 13, 19, 20 (bottom), 24, 25 (and border), 26 (bottom), 31, 33 (bottom), 34, 35, 36 (bottom), 38 (top and bottom), 39 (bottom), 42 (and border), 43, 44 (top), 46 (left), 49 (border) 50, 51, 64

Bridgeman Art Library, London: 1, 7 (top), 11, 16, 17 (top), 20 (top left), 21 (right), 22, 23 (bottom), 27, 30, 32 (top), 39 (top), 40, 41, 42, 45, 46 (top and bottom right), 47, 48, 52-53, 54-55, 57

British Library: 29 (top and bottom)

British Museum Publications, London: 44

Canterbury Museums © , Canterbury: 7, 9

Ebury Press, London: 17 (bottom)

E.T. Archive, London: 6

Sonia Halliday: 4, 56

Henry E. Huntington Art Library: 5, 15 (top), 18, 20 (top right), 21 (right), 26 (top), 28 (top right), 33 (top), 36 (top), 49 (bottom right)

© Scala Books, London: 55

Front cover: Lydgate Pilgrims leaving Canterbury. The Story of Thebes by John Lydgate. Reproduced by permission of the British Library.

Page 1 Chaucer. Page 2 Gough map - earliest known road map of Britain, detail of Kent showing road between Canterbury and London. Page 3 Pilgrim meets Pride who is carried on the shoulders of Flattery who holds a mirror. Page 4 Pilgrims. Canterbury Trinity Chapel. Page 5 Chaucer with pen-case, about to tell the tale of Melibee. Ellesmere.

References in the captions to Ellesmere refer to the Ellesmere Manuscript.

Comprehended in this litel tretys heere
To enforce with theffect of my matere
And though I nat the same wordes seye
As ye han herd, yet to yow alle I preye
Blameth me nat; for as in my sentence
Shul ye nowher fynden difference
Fro the sentence of this tretys lyte
After the which this murye tale I write
And therfore herkneth what þt I shal seye
And lat me tellen al my tale I preye

℩ Explicit ℩

℩ Heere biginneth Chaucers tale of Melibee

A yong man called Melibeus myghty and riche bigat
vp on his wyf that called was Prudence a doghter
which that called was Sophie. vpon a day bifel þt
he for his desport is went in to the feeldes hym to pleye
his wyf and eek his doghter hath he left withinne his hous of which
the dores weren faste yshette. thre of hise olde foes han it espyed
and setten laddres to the walles of his hous and by wyndowes
been entred and betten his wyf and wounded his doghter with
fyue mortal woundes in fyue sondry places. this is to seyn in
hir feet. in hir handes. in hir erys. in hir nose. and in hir mouth
and leften hir for deed and wenten awey ℩ whan Melibeus re-
torned was in to his hous and saugh al this meschief he lyk a
mad man rentynge his clothes gan to wepe and crie ℩ Pru-
dence his wyf as ferforth as she dorste bisoghte hym of his wepyng
for to stynte but nat for thy he gan to crie and wepen euere lenger
the moore ℩ This noble wyf Prudence remembred hir vpon this
sentence of Ouide in his book that cleped is the remedie of loue.
Wher as he seith he is a fool that destourbeth the mooder to wepen in
the deeth of hir child til she haue wept hir fille as for a certein
tyme. And thanne shal man doon his diligence with amyable
wordes hir to reconforte. and preyen hir of hir wepyng for to
stynte. ffor which reson this noble wyf Prudence suffred hir
housbonde for to wepe and crie as for a certein space. And whan
she saugh hir tyme she seyde hym in this wise. Allas my
lord quod she why make ye youre self for to be lyk a fool for to
the it apperteneth nat to a wys man to maken swich a sorwe yow

Labour of the month: April

Here bygynneth
the Book of the Tales of Caunterbury

Portrait of Chaucer
in Hoccleve's
Regement of Princes

Whan that Aprill with his shoures soote
The droghte of March hath perced to the roote,
And bathed every veyne in swich licour
Of which vertu engendred is the flour;
Whan Zephirus eek with his sweete breeth ⁵
Inspired hath in every holt and heeth
The tendre croppes, and the yonge sonne
Hath in the Ram his half cours yronne,
And smale foweles maken melodye,
That slepen al the nyght with open ye ¹⁰
(So priketh hem nature in hir corages),
Thanne longen folk to goon on pilgrimages,

*The Canterbury
Pilgrims by Paul
Hardy in
Canterbury
Museums ©*

Packhorse and driver approach Inn

And palmeres for to seken straunge strondes,
To ferne halwes, kowthe in sondry londes;
And specially from every shires ende 15
Of Engelond to Caunterbury they wende,
The hooly blisful martir for to seke,
That hem hath holpen whan that they were seeke.

Bifil that in that seson on a day,
In Southwerk at the Tabard as I lay 20
Redy to wenden on my pilgrymage
To Caunterbury with ful devout corage,
At nyght was come into that hostelrye
Wel nyne and twenty in a compaignye
Of sondry folk, by aventure yfalle 25
In felaweshipe, and pilgrimes were they alle,
That toward Caunterbury wolden ryde.
The chambres and the stables weren wyde,
And wel we weren esed atte beste.
And shortly, whan the sonne was to reste, 30
So hadde I spoken with hem everichon
That I was of hir felaweshipe anon,
And made forward erly for to ryse,
To take oure wey ther as I yow devyse.

The Prologue to the Canterbury Tales by Mortimer in Canterbury Museums ©

But nathelees, whil I have tyme and space, 35
Er that I ferther in this tale pace,
Me thynketh it acordaunt to resoun
To telle yow al the condicioun
Of ech of hem, so as it semed me,
And whiche they weren, and of what degree, 40
And eek in what array that they were inne;
And at a knyght than wol I first bigynne.

 KNYGHT ther was, and that a worthy man,
That fro the tyme that he first bigan
To riden out, he loved chivalrie, 45
Trouthe and honour, fredom and curteisie.
Ful worthy was he in his lordes werre,
And therto hadde he riden, no man ferre,
As wel in cristendom as in hethenesse,
And evere honoured for his worthynesse; 50
At Alisaundre he was whan it was wonne.
Ful ofte tyme he hadde the bord bigonne
Aboven alle nacions in Pruce;
In Lettow hadde he reysed and in Ruce,

*Left
Knight on
crusade.
From Les Très
Riches Heures du
Duc de Berry*

*Right
The Knight,
here in
civilian dress.
Ellesmere*

Iamque domos patrias Scithice post aspera gentis
prelia laurigero &c.

Here bigynneth the knyghtes tale

Whilom as olde stories tellen vs
Ther was a duc þt highte Theseus
Of Atthenes he was lord and gouernour
And in his tyme swich a conquerour
That gretter was ther noon vnder the sonne
Ful many a riche contree hadde he wonne
What with his wysdom and his chiualrie
He conquered al the regne of ffemenye
That whilom was ycleped Scithia
And wedded the queene ypolita
And broghte hir hoom wt hym in his contree
With muchel glorie and greet solempnytee
And eek hir faire suster Emelye
And thus with victorie and with melodye
Lete I this noble duc to Atthenes ryde
And al his hoost in armes hym bisyde
And certes if it were to long to heere
I wolde yow haue toold fully the manere
How wonnen was the regne of ffemenye
By Theseus and by his chiualrie
And of the grete bataille for the nones
Bitwixen Atthenes and Amazones
And how asseged was ypolita
The faire hardy queene of Scithia
And of the feste þt was at hir weddynge
And of the tempest at hir hoom comynge
But al that thyng I moot as now forbere
I haue god woot a large feeld to ere
And wayke been the oxen in my plough
The remenant of the tale is long ynough
I wol nat letten eek noon of this route
Lat euery felawe telle his tale aboute
And lat se now who shal the soper wynne
And ther I lefte I wol ayeyn bigynne

Narrat

This duc of whom I make mencioun
Whan he was come almoost on to the toun
In al his wele and in his mooste pride
He was war as he caste his eye a side
Where that ther kneled in the weye
A compaignye of ladyes tweye and tweye

No Cristen man so ofte of his degree. 55

In Gernade at the seege eek hadde he be

Of Algezir, and riden in Belmarye.

At Lyeys was he and at Satalye,

Whan they were wonne, and in the Grete See

At many a noble armee hadde he be. 60

At mortal batailles hadde he been fiftene,

And foughten for oure feith at Tramyssene

In lystes thries, and ay slayn his foo.

Right
Tournament

Knights
in
battle

12

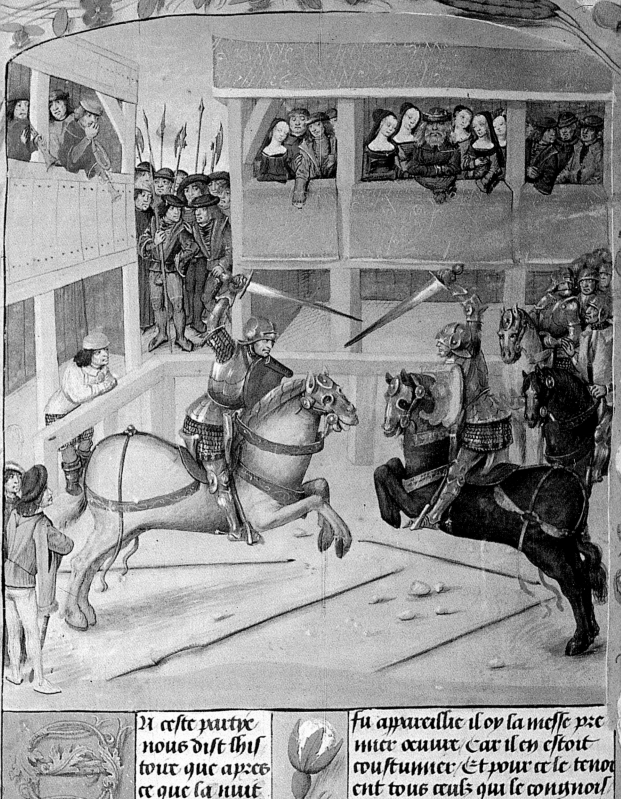

A ceste partie
nous dist lhis
toire que apres
ce que la nuit
du tournoiement

fu passee et que ce nuit a sen

fu appareillie il oy la messe pre
mier œuure car il en estoit
coustumier Et pour ce le tenoy
ent tous ceulx qui le congnoi
soient a moult preudomme tan
tost que la messe fu ditte et que

Knights in battle

This ilke worthy knyght hadde been also
Somtyme with the lord of Palatye   65
Agayn another hethen in Turkye;
And everemoore he hadde a sovereyn prys.
And though that he were worthy, he was wys,
And of his port as meeke as is a mayde.
He nevere yet no vileynye ne sayde   70
In al his lyf unto no maner wight.
He was a verray, parfit gentil knyght.
But for to tellen yow of his array,
His hors were goode, but he was nat gay.
Of fustian he wered a gypon   75
Al bismotered with his habergeon,
For he was late ycome from his viage,
And wente for to doon his pilgrymage.

With hym ther was his sone, a yong S Q U I E R ,
A lovyere and a lusty bacheler, 80
With lokkes crulle as they were leyd in presse.
Of twenty yeer of age he was, I gesse.
Of his stature he was of evene lengthe,
And wonderly delyvere, and of greet strengthe.
And he hadde been somtyme in chyvachie 85
In Flaundres, in Artoys, and Pycardie,
And born hym weel, as of so litel space,
In hope to stonden in his lady grace.
Embrouded was he, as it were a meede
Al ful of fresshe floures, whyte and reede. 90
Syngynge he was, or floytynge, al the day;

The Squire
Ellesmere

Romance
of the
Rose.
The lover
asks
Richesse
the way

He was as fressh as is the month of May.

Short was his gowne, with sleves longe and wyde.

Wel koude he sitte on hors and faire ryde.

He koude songes make and wel endite, 95

Juste and eek daunce, and weel purtreye and write.

So hoote he lovede that by nyghtertale

He sleep namoore than dooth a nyghtyngale.

Curteis he was, lowely, and servysable,

And carf biforn his fader at the table. 100

Emilia in her garden watched by prisoners

A Yeman hadde he and servantz namo
   At that tyme, for hym liste ride so,
      And he was clad in cote and hood of grene.
   A sheef of pecok arwes, bright and kene,
   Under his belt he bar ful thriftily   105
   (Wel koude he dresse his takel yemanly;
   His arwes drouped noght with fetheres lowe),
   And in his hand he baar a myghty bowe.
   A not heed hadde he, with a broun visage.
   Of wodecraft wel koude he al the usage.   110
   Upon his arm he baar a gay bracer,
   And by his syde a swerd and a bokeler,
   And on that oother syde a gay daggere
   Harneised wel and sharp as point of spere;
   A Cristopher on his brest of silver sheene.   115
   An horn he bar, the bawdryk was of grene;
   A forster was he, soothly, as I gesse.

The Yeoman
Ellesmere

Yeoman with bow

Ther was also a Nonne, a PRIORESSE,
That of hir smylyng was ful symple and coy;
Hire gretteste ooth was but by Seinte Loy;   120
And she was cleped madame Eglentyne.
Ful weel she soong the service dyvyne,
Entuned in hir nose ful semely;
And Frenssh she spak ful faire and fetisly,
After the scole of Stratford atte Bowe,   125
For Frenssh of Parys was to hire unknowe.
At mete wel ytaught was she with alle;
She leet no morsel from hir lippes falle,
Ne wette hir fyngres in hir sauce depe;
Wel koude she carie a morsel and wel kepe   130
That no drope ne fille upon hire brest.
In curteisie was set ful muchel hir lest.
Hir over-lippe wyped she so clene
That in hir coppe ther was no ferthyng sene
Of grece, whan she dronken hadde hir draughte.   135
Ful semely after hir mete she raughte.
And sikerly she was of greet desport,
And ful plesaunt, and amyable of port,
And peyned hire to countrefete cheere
Of court, and to been estatlich of manere,   140
And to ben holden digne of reverence.
But for to speken of hire conscience,
She was so charitable and so pitous
She wolde wepe, if that she saugh a mous
Kaught in a trappe, if it were deed or bledde.   145
Of smale houndes hadde she that she fedde
With rosted flessh, or milk and wastel-breed.
But soore wepte she if oon of hem were deed,
Or if men smoot it with a yerde smerte;
And al was conscience and tendre herte.   150
Ful semyly hir wympul pynched was,

The Prioress,
side-saddle,
with rosary.
Ellesmere

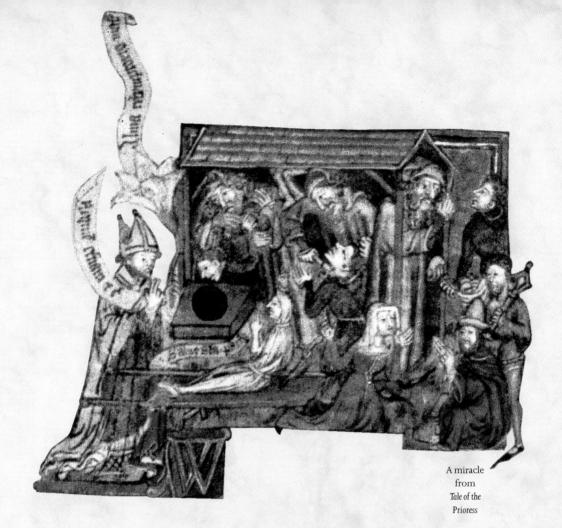

A miracle
from
*Tale of the
Prioress*

Hir nose tretys, hir eyen greye as glas,
Hir mouth ful smal, and therto softe and reed.
But sikerly she hadde a fair forheed;
It was almoost a spanne brood, I trowe;   155
For, hardily, she was nat undergrowe.
Ful fetys was hir cloke, as I was war.
Of smal coral aboute hire arm she bar
A peire of bedes, gauded al with grene,
And theron heng a brooch of gold ful sheene,   160
On which ther was first write a crowned A,
And after *Amor vincit omnia.*

Nun

The Nun's Priest.
Ellesmere

Another NONNE with hire hadde she,
That was hir chapeleyne, and preestes thre.

Priest at a burial

A MONK ther was, a fair for the maistrie, 165
An outridere, that lovede venerie,
A manly man, to been an abbot able.
Ful many a deyntee hors hadde he in stable,
And whan he rood, men myghte his brydel heere
Gynglen in a whistlynge wynd als cleere 170
And eek as loude as dooth the chapel belle
Ther as this lord was kepere of the celle.
The reule of Seint Maure or of Seint Beneit—
By cause that it was old and somdel streit
This ilke Monk leet olde thynges pace, 175
And heeld after the newe world the space.
He yaf nat of that text a pulled hen,
That seith that hunters ben nat hooly men,
Ne that a monk, whan he is recchelees,
Is likned til a fissh that is waterlees— 180
This is to seyn, a monk out of his cloystre.
But thilke text heeld he nat worth an oystre;
And I seyde his opinion was good.
What sholde he studie and make hymselven wood,
Upon a book in cloystre alwey to poure, 185
Or swynken with his handes, and laboure,
As Austyn bit? How shal the world be served?
Lat Austyn have his swynk to hym reserved!
Therfore he was a prikasour aright:
Grehoundes he hadde as swift as fowel in flight; 190
Of prikyng and of huntyng for the hare
Was al his lust, for no cost wolde he spare.
I seigh his sleves purfiled at the hond
With grys, and that the fyneste of a lond;
And for to festne his hood under his chyn, 195
He hadde of gold ywroght a ful curious pyn;
A love-knotte in the gretter ende ther was.
His heed was balled, that shoon as any glas,

The Monk,
with bells
on bridle.
Ellesmere

Hunting.
One of three
elements of a
hunting scene
to be found in
the intrusive
panels in
Westminster
Abbey Chapter
House, paved
by 1258.
Drawn by
Rosamund
Nairac.

The Monk's
hunting dogs.
Ellesmere

21

Labour of December: the Boar Hunt from *Les Très Riches Heures du Duc de Berry*

And eek his face, as he hadde been enoynt.

He was a lord ful fat and in good poynt; 200

His eyen stepe, and rollynge in his heed,

That stemed as a forneys of a leed;

His bootes souple, his hors in greet estaat.

Now certeinly he was a fair prelaat;

He was nat pale as a forpyned goost. 205

A fat swan loved he best of any roost.

His palfrey was as broun as is a berye.

A FRERE ther was, a wantowne and a merye,

A lymytour, a ful solempne man.

In alle the ordres foure is noon that kan 210

So muchel of daliaunce and fair langage.

He hadde maad ful many a mariage

Of yonge wommen at his owene cost.

Unto his ordre he was a noble post.

Ful wel biloved and famulier was he 215

With frankeleyns over al in his contree,

And eek with worthy wommen of the toun;

For he hadde power of confessioun,

As seyde hymself, moore than a curat,

For of his ordre he was licenciat. 220

Ful swetely herde he confessioun,

And plesaunt was his absolucion:

He was an esy man to yeve penaunce,

Ther as he wiste to have a good pitaunce,

For unto a povre ordre for to yive 225

Is signe that a man is wel yshryve;

For if he yaf, he dorste make avaunt,

He wiste that a man was repentaunt;

For many a man so hard is of his herte,

He may nat wepe, althogh hym soore smerte. 230

Therfore in stede of wepynge and preyeres

And olde and myrry nyght
God send hem sone very ioy

Here
And

Hit

he may
Vpon
No w
But

Men moote yeve silver to the povre freres.

His typet was ay farsed ful of knyves

And pynnes, for to yeven faire wyves.

And certeinly he hadde a murye note: 235

Wel koude he synge and pleyen on a rote;

Of yeddynges he baar outrely the pris.

His nekke whit was as the flour-de-lys;

Therto he strong was as a champioun.

He knew the tavernes wel in every toun 240

And everich hostiler and tappestere

Bet than a lazar or a beggestere,

For unto swich a worthy man as he

Acorded nat, as by his facultee,

To have with sike lazars aqueyntaunce. 245

It is nat honest; it may nat avaunce,

For to deelen with no swich poraille,

But al with riche and selleres of vitaille.

And over al, ther as profit sholde arise,

Curteis he was and lowely of servyse; 250

Ther nas no man nowher so vertuous.

He was the beste beggere in his hous;

[And yaf a certeyn ferme for the graunt; 252a

Noon of his bretheren cam ther in his haunt;] 252b

For thogh a wydwe hadde noght a sho,

So plesaunt was his *"In principio,"*

Yet wolde he have a ferthyng, er he wente. 255

His purchas was wel bettre than his rente.

And rage he koude, as it were right a whelp.

In love-dayes ther koude he muchel help,

For ther he was nat lyk a cloysterer

With a thredbare cope, as is a povre scoler, 260

But he was lyk a maister or a pope.

Of double worstede was his semycope,

That rounded as a belle out of the presse.

Somwhat he lipsed, for his wantownesse,

To make his Englissh sweete upon his tonge; 265

And in his harpyng, whan that he hadde songe,

His eyen twynkled in his heed aryght

As doon the sterres in the frosty nyght.

This worthy lymytour was cleped Huberd.

A MARCHANT was ther with a forked berd, 270

In mottelee, and hye on horse he sat;

Upon his heed a Flaundryssh bever hat,

His bootes clasped faire and fetisly.

His resons he spak ful solempnely,

Sownynge alwey th'encrees of his wynnyng. 275

He wolde the see were kept for any thyng

Bitwixe Middelburgh and Orewelle.

Wel koude he in eschaunge sheeldes selle.

This worthy man ful wel his wit bisette:

Ther wiste no wight that he was in dette, 280

The Merchant, on a lively horse.
Ellesmere

So estatly was he of his governaunce
With his bargaynes and with his chevyssaunce.
For sothe he was a worthy man with alle,
But, sooth to seyn, I noot how men hym calle.

A CLERK ther was of Oxenford also, 285
That unto logyk hadde longe ygo.
As leene was his hors as is a rake,
And he nas nat right fat, I undertake,
But looked holwe, and therto sobrely.
Ful thredbare was his overeste courtepy, 290
For he hadde geten hym yet no benefice,
Ne was so worldly for to have office.
For hym was levere have at his beddes heed
Twenty bookes, clad in blak or reed,
Of Aristotle and his philosophie 295
Than robes riche, or fithele, or gay sautrie.
But al be that he was a philosophre,
Yet hadde he but litel gold in cofre;
But al that he myghte of his freendes hente,
On bookes and on lernynge he it spente, 300
And bisily gan for the soules preye
Of hem that yaf hym wherwith to scoleye.
Of studie took he moost cure and moost heede.
Noght o word spak he moore than was neede,
And that was seyd in forme and reverence, 305
And short and quyk and ful of hy sentence;
Sownynge in moral vertu was his speche,
And gladly wolde he lerne and gladly teche.

The Clerk with book,
on his lean horse.
Ellesmere

A SERGEANT OF THE LAWE, war and wys,
That often hadde been at the Parvys, 310
Ther was also, ful riche of excellence.
Discreet he was and of greet reverence—

He semed swich, his wordes weren so wise.
Justice he was ful often in assise,
By patente and by pleyn commissioun.   315
For his science and for his heigh renoun,
Of fees and robes hadde he many oon.
So greet a purchasour was nowher noon:
Al was fee symple to hym in effect;
His purchasyng myghte nat been infect.   320
Nowher so bisy a man as he ther nas,
And yet he semed bisier than he was.
In termes hadde he caas and doomes alle
That from the tyme of kyng William were falle.
Therto he koude endite and make a thyng,   325
Ther koude no wight pynche at his writyng;
And every statut koude he pleyn by rote.
He rood but hoomly in a medlee cote,
Girt with a ceint of silk, with barres smale;
Of his array telle I no lenger tale.   330

The Sergeant
of the Law.
Ellesmere

A FRANKELEYN was in his compaignye.
Whit was his berd as is the dayesye;
Of his complexioun he was sangwyn.
Wel loved he by the morwe a sop in wyn;
To lyven in delit was evere his wone,   335
For he was Epicurus owene sone,
That heeld opinioun that pleyn delit
Was verray felicitee parfit.
An housholdere, and that a greet, was he;
Seint Julian he was in his contree.   340
His breed, his ale, was alweys after oon;
A bettre envyned man was nowher noon.
Withoute bake mete was nevere his hous,
Of fissh and flessh, and that so plentevous
It snewed in his hous of mete and drynke;   345

Of all deyntees that men koude thynke;
After the sondry sesons of the yeer,
So chaunged he his mete and his soper.
Ful many a fat partrich hadde he in muwe,
And many a breem and many a luce in stuwe. 350
Wo was his cook but if his sauce were
Poynaunt and sharp, and redy al his geere.
His table dormant in his halle alway
Stood redy covered al the longe day.
At sessiouns ther was he lord and sire; 355
Ful ofte tyme he was knyght of the shire.
An anlaas and a gipser al of silk

Man killing pig

Pouring wine
into vats under
supervision

The Franklin.
Ellesmere

Heeng at his girdel, whit as morne milk.
A shirreve hadde he been, and a contour.
Was nowher swich a worthy vavasour.   360

AN HABERDASSHERE and a CARPENTER,
A WEBBE, a DYERE, and a TAPYCER—
And they were clothed alle in o lyveree
Of a solempne and a greet fraternitee.
Ful fressh and newe hir geere apiked was;   365
Hir knyves were chaped noght with bras
But al with silver, wroght ful clene and weel,
Hire girdles and hir pouches everydeel.
Wel semed ech of hem a fair burgeys
To sitten in a yeldehalle on a deys.   370
Everich, for the wisdom that he kan,
Was shaply for to been an alderman.
For catel hadde they ynogh and rente,
And eek hir wyves wolde it wel assente;
And elles certeyn were they to blame.   375
It is ful fair to been ycleped "madame,"
And goon to vigilies al bifore,
And have a mantel roialliche ybore.

Burghers
surrender the
keys of their city

A Cook they hadde with hem for the nones
To boille the chiknes with the marybones,   380
And poudre-marchant tart and galyngale.
Wel koude he knowe a draughte of Londoun ale.
He koude rooste, and sethe, and broille, and frye,
Maken mortreux, and wel bake a pye.
But greet harm was it, as it thoughte me,   385
That on his shyne a mormal hadde he.
For blankmanger, that made he with the beste.

The Cook, with meat-hook. *Ellesmere*

A feast
out of
doors

32

A SHIPMAN was ther, wonynge fer by weste;
For aught I woot, he was of Dertemouthe.
He rood upon a rouncy, as he kouthe,   390
In a gowne of faldyng to the knee.
A daggere hangynge on a laas hadde he
Aboute his nekke, under his arm adoun.
The hoote somer hadde maad his hewe al broun;
And certeinly he was a good felawe.   395
Ful many a draughte of wyn had he ydrawe

The
Shipman,
with
dagger.
Ellesmere

Shipwreck

Ship and
Whale

Fro Burdeux-ward, whil that the chapman sleep.

Of nyce conscience took he no keep.

If that he faught and hadde the hyer hond,

By water he sente hem hoom to every lond. 400

But of his craft to rekene wel his tydes,

His stremes, and his daungers hym bisides,

His herberwe, and his moone, his lodemenage,

Ther nas noon swich from Hulle to Cartage.

Hardy he was and wys to undertake; 405

With many a tempest hadde his berd been shake.

He knew alle the havenes, as they were,

Fro Gootlond to the cape of Fynystere,

And every cryke in Britaigne and in Spayne.

His barge ycleped was the Maudelayne 410

Loading a ship

With us ther was a DOCTOUR OF PHISIK;
In al this world ne was ther noon hym lik,
To speke of phisik and of surgerye,
For he was grounded in astronomye.
He kepte his pacient a ful greet deel   415
In houres by his magyk natureel.
Wel koude he fortunen the ascendent
Of his ymages for his pacient.
He knew the cause of everich maladye,
Were it of hoot, or coold, or moyste, or drye,   420
And where they engendred, and of what humour.

The Doctor,
with phial.
Ellesmere

Eye-
surgery

Albule oculorum sic excu
tuntur;

He was a verray, parfit praktisour:
The cause yknowe, and of his harm the roote,
Anon he yaf the sike man his boote.
Ful redy hadde he his apothecaries   425
To sende hym drogges and his letuaries,
For ech of hem made oother for to wynne—
Hir frendshipe nas nat newe to bigynne.
Wel knew he the olde Esculapius,
And Deyscorides, and eek Rufus,   430
Olde Ypocras, Haly, and Galyen,

Physicians
and a
swooning
lady

Serapion, Razis, and Avycen,

Averrois, Damascien, and Constantyn,

Bernard, and Gatesden, and Gilbertyn.

Of his diete mesurable was he,   435

For it was no superfluitee,

But of greet norissyng and digestible.

His studie was but litel on the Bible.

In sangwyn and in pers he clad was al,

Lyned with taffata and with sendal.   440

And yet he was but esy of dispence;

He kepte that he wan in pestilence.

For gold in phisik is a cordial,

Therefore he lovede gold in special.

Zodiacal figure

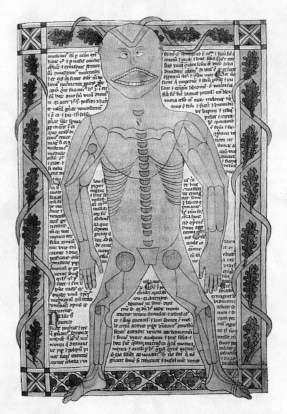

Diagram
of body

38

A good WIF was ther OF biside BATHE,   445
 But she was somdel deef, and that was scathe.
  Of clooth-makyng she hadde swich an haunt
She passed hem of Ypres and of Gaunt.
In al the parisshe wif ne was ther noon
That to the offrynge bifore hire sholde goon;   450
And if ther dide, certeyn so wrooth was she
That she was out of all charitee.
Hir coverchiefs ful fyne weren of ground;
I dorste swere they weyeden ten pound
That on a Sonday weren upon hir heed.   455
Hir hosen weren of fyn scarlet reed,

The Wife of Bath, with whip. *Ellesmere*

Priest
celebrates
marriage at
church
door

39

Ful streite yteyd, and shoes ful moyste and newe.

Boold was hir face, and fair, and reed of hewe.

She was a worthy womman al hir lyve:

Housbondes at chirche door she hadde fyve,   460

Withouten oother compaignye in youthe—

But thereof nedeth nat to speke as nowthe.

And thries hadde she been at Jerusalem;

She hadde passed many a straunge strem;

At Rome she hadde been, and at Boloigne,   465

In Galice at Seint-Jame, and at Coloigne.

She koude muchel of wandrynge by the weye.

Gat-tothed was she, soothly for to seye.

Upon an amblere esily she sat,

Ywympled wel, and on hir heed an hat   470

As brood as is a bokeler or a targe;

A foot-mantel aboute hir hipes large,

And on hir feet a paire of spores sharpe.

In felaweshipe wel koude she laughe and carpe.

Of remedies of love she knew per chaunce,   475

For she koude of that art the olde daunce.

A good man was ther of religioun,
And was a povre PERSOUN OF A TOUN,
But riche he was of hooly thoght and werk.
He was also a lerned man, a clerk, 480
That Cristes gospel trewely wolde preche;
His parisshens devoutly wolde he teche.
Benygne he was, and wonder diligent,
And in adversitee ful pacient,
And swich he was ypreved ofte sithes. 485
Ful looth were hym to cursen for his tithes,
But rather wolde he yeven, out of doute,
Unto his povre parisshens aboute
Of his offryng and eek of his substaunce.
He koude in litel thyng have suffisaunce. 490
Wyd was his parisshe, and houses fer asonder,
But he ne lefte nat, for reyn ne thonder,
In siknesse nor in meschief to visite
The ferreste in his parisshe, muche and lite,
Upon his feet, and in his hand a staf. 495
This noble ensample to his sheep he yaf,
That first he wroghte, and afterward he taughte.
Out of the gospel he tho wordes caughte,
And this figure he added eek therto,
That if gold ruste, what shal iren do? 500
For if a preest be foul, on whom we truste,
No wonder is a lewed man to ruste;
And shame it is, if a prest take keep,
A shiten shepherde and a clene sheep.
Wel oghte a preest ensample for to yive, 505
By his clennesse, how that his sheep sholde lyve.
He sette nat his benefice to hyre
And leet his sheep encombred in the myre
And ran to Londoun unto Seinte Poules
To seken hym a chaunterie for soules, 510

The village
Parson.
Ellesmere

42

Or with a bretherhed to been withholde;

But dwelte at hoom, and kepte wel his folde,

So that the wolf ne made it nat myscarie;

He was a shepherde and noght a mercenarie.

And though he hooly were and vertuous,   515

He was to synful men nat despitous,

Ne of his speche daungerous ne digne,

But in his techyng discreet and benygne.

To drawen folk to hevene by fairnesse,

By good ensample, this was his bisynesse.   520

But it were any persone obstinat,

What so he were, of heigh or lough estat,

Hym wolde he snybben sharply for the nonys.

A bettre preest I trowe that nowher noon ys.

He waited after no pompe and reverence,   525

Ne maked him a spiced conscience,

But Cristes loore and his apostles twelve

He taughte; but first he folwed it hymselve.

Reason
preaching
in the
pulpit

With hym ther was a PLOWMAN, was his brother,
That hadde ylad of dong ful many a fother; 530
A trewe swynkere and a good was he,
Lyvynge in pees and parfit charitee.
God loved he best with al his hoole herte
At alle tymes, thogh him gamed or smerte,
And thanne his neighebor right as hymselve. 535
He wolde thresshe, and therto dyke and delve,
For Cristes sake, for every povre wight,
Withouten hire, if it lay in his myght.
His tithes payde he ful faire and wel,
Bothe of his propre swynk and his catel. 540
In a tabard he rood upon a mere.

Worker with spade and horn

Repairing
the
plough-
beam

Right
Ploughing,
from
*Les Très Riches
Heures du
Duc de Berry*

44

Ther was also a REVE, and a MILLERE,
A SOMNOUR, and a PARDONER also,
A MAUNCIPLE, and myself—ther were namo.

The MILLERE was a stout carl for the nones; 545
Ful byg he was of brawn, and eek of bones.
That proved wel, for over al ther he cam,
At wrastlynge he wolde have alwey the ram.
He was short-sholdred, brood, a thikke knarre;
Ther was no dore that he nolde heve of harre, 550
Or breke it at a rennyng with his heed.
His berd as any sowe or fox was reed,
And therto brood, as though it were a spade.
Upon the cop right of his nose he hade
A werte, and theron stood a toft of herys, 555
Reed as the brustles of a sowes erys;
His nosethirles blake were and wyde.
A swerd and a bokeler bar he by his syde.
His mouth as greet was as a greet forneys.
He was a janglere and a goliardeys, 560
And that was moost of synne and harlotries.
Wel koude he stelen corn and tollen thries;
And yet he hadde a thombe of gold, pardee.
A whit cote and a blew hood wered he.
A baggepipe wel koude he blowe and sowne, 565
And therwithal he broghte us out of towne.

A gentil MAUNCIPLE was ther of a Temple,
Of which achatours myghte take exemple
For to be wise in byynge of vitaille;
For wheither that he payde or took by taille, 570
Algate he wayted so in his achaat
That he was ay biforn and in good staat.
Now is nat that of God a ful fair grace

The Manciple
of a Temple

The Miller.
Ellesmere

That swich a lewed mannes wit shal pace
The wisdom of an heep of lerned men? 575
Of maistres hadde he mo than thries ten,
That weren of lawe expert and curious,
Of which ther were a duszeyne in that hous
Worthy to been stywardes of rente and lond
Of any lord that is in Engelond, 580
To make hym lyve by his propre good
In honour dettelees (but if he were wood),
Or lyve as scarsly as hym list desire;
And able for to helpen al a shire
In any caas that myghte falle or happe. 585
And yet this Manciple sette hir aller cappe.

The Reeve
Ellesmere

The REVE was a sclendre colerik man.
His berd was shave as ny as ever he kan;
His heer was by his erys ful round yshorn;
His top was dokked lyk a preest biforn. 590
Ful longe were his legges and ful lene,
Ylyk a staf; ther was no calf ysene.
Wel koude he kepe a gerner and a bynne;
Ther was noon auditour koude on him wynne.
Ther wiste he by the droghte and by the reyn 595
The yeldynge of his seed and of his greyn.
His lordes sheep, his neet, his dayerye,
His swyn, his hors, his stoor, and his pultrye
Was hoolly in this Reves governynge,
And by his convenant yaf the rekenynge, 600
Syn that his lord was twenty yeer of age.
Ther koude no man brynge hym in arrerage.
Ther nas baillif, ne hierde, nor oother hyne,
That he ne knew his sleighte and his covyne;
They were adrad of hym as of the deeth. 605
His wonyng was ful faire upon an heeth;

Sheep

47

With grene trees yshadwed was his place.

He koude bettre than his lord purchace.

Ful riche he was astored pryvely.

His lord wel koude he plesen subtilly, 610

To yeve and lene hym of his owene good,

And have a thank, and yet a cote and hood.

In youthe he hadde lerned a good myster:

He was a wel good wrighte, a carpenter.

This Reve sat upon a ful good stot 615

That was al pomely grey and highte Scot.

A long surcote of pers upon he hade,

And by his syde he baar a rusty blade.

Of Northfolk was this Reve of which I telle,

Biside a toun men clepen Baldeswelle. 620

Tukked he was as is a frere aboute,

And evere he rood the hyndreste of oure route.

A SOMONOUR was ther with us in that place,
That hadde a fyr-reed cherubynnes face,
For saucefleem he was, with eyen narwe. 625

As hoot he was and lecherous as a sparwe,

With scalled browes blake and piled berd.

Of his visage children were aferd.

Ther nas quyk-silver, lytarge, ne brymstoon,

Boras, ceruce, ne oille of tartre noon, 630

Ne oynement that wolde clense and byte,

That hym myghte helpen of his whelkes white,

Nor of the knobbes sittynge on his chekes.

Wel loved he garleek, oynons, and eek lekes,

And for to drynken strong wyn, reed as blood; 635

Thanne wolde he speke and crie as he were wood.

And whan that he wel dronken hadde the wyn,

Thanne wolde he speke no word but Latyn.

A fewe termes hadde he, two or thre,

The Summoner,
holding a writ.
Ellesmere

That he had lerned out of som decree — 640
No wonder is, he herde it al the day;
And eek ye knowen wel how that a jay
Kan clepen "Watte" as wel as kan the pope.
But whoso koude in oother thyng hym grope,
Thanne hadde he spent al his philosophie; 645
Ay "*Questio quid iuris*" wolde he crie.
He was a gentil harlot and a kynde;
A bettre felawe sholde men noght fynde.
He wolde suffre for a quart of wyn
A good felawe to have his concubyn 650
A twelf month, and excuse hym atte fulle;
Ful prively a fynch eek koude he pulle.
And if he foond owher a good felawe,
He wolde techen him to have noon awe
In swich caas of the ercedekenes curs, 655
But if a mannes soule were in his purs;
For in his purs he sholde ypunysshed be.
"Purs is the ercedekenes helle," seyde he.
But wel I woot he lyed right in dede;
Of cursyng oghte ech gilty man him drede, 660
For curs wol slee right as assoillyng savith,
And also war hym of a *Significavit*.
In daunger hadde he at his owene gise
The yonge girles of the diocise,
And knew hir conseil, and was al hir reed. 665
A gerland hadde he set upon his heed,
As greet as it were for an ale-stake.
A bokeleer hadde he maad hym of a cake.

The Pardoner,
holding a cross.
Ellesmere

W
ith hym ther rood a gentil PARDONER
Of Rouncivale, his freend and his compeer, 670
That streight was comen fro the court of Rome.
Ful loude he soong "Com hider, love, to me!"

49

This Somonour bar to hym a stif burdoun;
Was nevere trompe of half so greet a soun.
This Pardoner hadde heer as yelow as wex,   675
But smothe it heeng as dooth a strike of flex;
By ounces henge his lokkes that he hadde,
And therwith he his shuldres overspradde;
But thynne it lay, by colpons oon and oon.
But hood, for jolitee, wered he noon,   680
For it was trussed up in his walet.
Hym thoughte he rood al of the newe jet;
Dischevelee, save his cappe, he rood al bare.
Swiche glarynge eyen hadde he as an hare.
A vernycle hadde he sowed upon his cappe.   685
His walet, biforn hym in his lappe,
Bretful of pardoun comen from Rome al hoot.
A voys he hadde as smal as hath a goot.
No berd hadde he, ne nevere sholde have;
As smothe it was as it were late shave.   690
I trowe he were a geldyng or a mare.
But of his craft, fro Berwyk into Ware
Ne was ther swich another pardoner.
For in his male he hadde a pilwe-beer,
Which that he seyde was Oure Lady veyl;   695
He seyde he hadde a gobet of the seyl
That Seint Peter hadde, whan that he wente
Upon the see, til Jhesu Crist hym hente.
He hadde a croys of latoun ful of stones,
And in a glas he hadde pigges bones.   700
But with thise relikes, whan that he fond
A povre person dwellynge upon lond,
Upon a day he gat hym moore moneye
Than that the person gat in monthes tweye;
And thus, with feyned flaterye and japes,   705
He made the person and the peple his apes.

Priest
holding
pardon

But trewely to tellen atte laste
He was in chirche a noble ecclesiaste.
Wel koude he rede a lessoun or a storie,
But alderbest he song an offertorie;   710
For wel he wiste, whan that song was songe,
He moste preche and wel affile his tonge
To wynne silver, as he ful wel koude;
Therefore he song the murierly and loude.

Now have I toold you soothly, in a clause,   715
Th'estaat, th'array, the nombre, and eek the cause
Why that assembled was this compaignye
In Southwerk at this gentil hostelrye

A man and
woman
talking

That highte the Tabard, faste by the Belle.

But now is tyme to yow for to telle   720

How that we baren us that ilke nyght,

Whan we were in that hostelrie alyght;

And after wol I telle of our viage

And al the remenaunt of oure pilgrimage.

But first I pray yow, of youre curteisye,   725

That ye n'arette it nat my vileynye,

Thogh that I pleynly speke in this mateere,

To telle yow hir wordes and hir cheere,

Ne thogh I speke hir wordes proprely.

For this ye knowen al so wel as I: 730

Webster's
Pilgrims

Whoso shal telle a tale after a man,

He moot reherce as ny as evere he kan

Everich a word, if it be in his charge,

Al speke he never so rudeliche and large,

Or ellis he moot telle his tale untrewe,   735

Or feyne thyng, or fynde wordes newe.

He may nat spare, althogh he were his brother;

He moot as wel seye o word as another.

Crist spak hymself ful brode in hooly writ,

And wel ye woot no vileynye is it. 740
Eek Plato seith, whoso kan hym rede,
The wordes moote be cosyn to the dede.
Also I prey yow to foryeve it me,
Al have I nat set folk in hir degree
Heere in this tale, as that they sholde stonde. 745
My wit is short, ye may wel understonde.

Greet chiere made oure Hoost us everichon,
And to the soper sette he us anon.
He served us with vitaille at the beste;
Strong was the wyn, and wel to drynke us leste. 750

A semely man OURE HOOSTE was withalle
For to been a marchal in an halle.
A large man he was with eyen stepe—
A fairer burgeys was ther noon in Chepe—
Boold of his speche, and wys, and wel ytaught, 755
And of manhod hym lakkede right naught.
Eek therto he was right a myrie man;
And after soper pleyen he bigan,
And spak of myrthe amonges othere thynges,

Whan that we hadde maad oure rekenynges, 760
And seyde thus: "Now, lordynges, trewely,
Ye been to me right welcome, hertely;
For by my trouthe, if that I shal nat lye,
I saugh nat this yeer so myrie a compaignye
Atones in this herberwe as is now. 765
Fayn wolde I doon yow myrthe, wiste I how.
And of a myrthe I am right now bythoght,
To doon yow ese, and it shal coste noght.

"Ye goon to Caunterbury — God yow speede,
The blisful martir quite yow youre meede! 770
And wel I woot, as ye goon by the weye,
Ye shapen yow to talen and to pleye;
For trewely, confort ne myrthe is noon
To ride by the weye doumb as a stoon;
And therfore wol I maken yow disport, 775
As I seyde erst, and doon yow som confort.
And if yow liketh alle by oon assent
For to stonden at my juggement,
And for to werken as I shal yow seye,
Tomorwe, whan ye riden by the weye, 780
Now, by my fader soule that is deed,
But ye be myrie, I wol yeve yow myn heed!
Hoold up youre hondes, withouten moore speche."

A merry monk

Oure conseil was nat longe for to seche.
Us thoughte it was noght worth to make it wys, 785
And graunted hym withouten moore avys,
And bad him seye his voirdit as hym leste.
"Lordynges," quod he, "now herkneth for the beste;
But taak it nought, I prey yow, in desdeyn.
This is the poynt, to speken short and pleyn, 790
That ech of yow, to shorte with oure weye,

In this viage shal telle tales tweye
To Caunterbury-ward, I mene it so,
And homward he shal tellen othere two,
Of aventures that whilom han bifalle. 795
And which of yow that bereth hym best of alle—
That is to seyn, that telleth in this caas
Tales of best sentence and moost solaas—
Shal have a soper at oure aller cost
Heere in this place, sittynge by this post, 800
Whan that we come agayn fro Caunterbury.
And for to make yow the moore mury,
I wol myselven goodly with yow ryde,
Right at myn owene cost, and be youre gyde;
And whoso wole my juggement withseye 805
Shal paye al that we spenden by the weye.
And if ye vouche sauf that it be so,
Tel me anon, withouten wordes mo,
And I wol erly shape me therfore."

This thyng was graunted, and oure othes swore 810
With ful glad herte, and preyden hym also
That he wolde vouche sauf for to do so,
And that he wolde been oure governour,
And of oure tales juge and reportour,
And sette a soper at a certeyn pris, 815
And we wol reuled been at his devys
In heigh and lough; and thus by oon assent
We been acorded to his juggement.
And therupon the wyn was fet anon;
We dronken, and to reste wente echon, 820
Withouten any lenger taryynge.

Murder of
Becket,
Canterbury
Cathedral

Amorwe, whan that day bigan to sprynge,
Up roos oure Hoost, and was oure aller cok,
And gadrede us togidre alle in a flok,
And forth we riden a litel moore than paas   825
Unto the Wateryng of Seint Thomas;
And there oure Hoost bigan his hors areste
And seyde, "Lordynges, herkneth, if yow leste.
Ye woot youre foreward, and I it yow recorde.
If even-song and morwe-song accorde,   830
Lat se now who shal telle the firste tale.
As evere mote I drynke wyn or ale,
Whoso be rebel to my juggement
Shal paye for al that by the wey is spent.
Now draweth cut, er that we ferrer twynne;   835
He which that hath the shorteste shal bigynne.
Sire Knyght," quod he, "my mayster and my lord,
Now draweth cut, for that is myn accord.
Cometh neer," quod he, "my lady Prioresse.

And ye, sire Clerk, lat be youre shamefastnesse, 840
Ne studieth noght; ley hond to, every man!"
Anon to drawen every wight bigan,
And shortly for to tellen as it was,
Were it by aventure, or sort, or cas,
The sothe is this: the cut fil to the Knyght, 845
Of which ful blithe and glad was every wyght,
And telle he moste his tale, as was resoun,
By foreward and by composicioun,
As ye han herd; what nedeth wordes mo?
And whan this goode man saugh that it was so, 850
As he that wys was and obedient
To kepe his foreward by his free assent,
He seyde, "Syn I shal bigynne the game,
What, welcome by the cut, a Goddes name!
Now lat us ryde, and herkneth what I seye." 855
And with that word we ryden forth oure weye,
And we bigan with right a myrie cheere
His tale anon, and seyde as ye may heere.

Scott's Chaucer

NOTES FOR ILLUSTRATED PROLOGUE

Notes are keyed to line numbers. The meaning of unfamiliar words, expressions or lines is given first. Explanatory notes are in brackets.

1 *his* his, its *shoures soote* sweet showers

2 *droghte* dryness *perced* pierced

3 *veyne* vein of sap *swich licour* liquid such that

4 *Of which vertu* by its power *flour* flower

5 *Zephirus* god of west wind; breeze *eek* also

6 *inspired* breathed life into *holt* grove *heeth* field

7 *croppes* shoots, new leaves *yonge* young (The sun's year begins at the Spring equinox, then 12 March.)

8 Has run (the second) half of his course in Aries. (The sun completed his transit of Aries, first sign of the zodiac, on 11 April. Later in the *Tales* the date of 18 April is given.)

9 *smale foweles* little birds

10 *ye* eye (The birds are light sleepers.)

11 So much does Nature prick them in their hearts

12 *longen folk to goon* people long to go

13 *palmeres* pilgrims (from the palms carried by pilgrims to the Holy Land) *straunge strondes* foreign shores

14 *every shires ende* the corner of every county

16 *wende* make their way

17 *blisful martir* blessed martyr (Thomas Becket, Archbishop of Canterbury, killed at the altar of the cathedral by knights of Henry II in 1170; his shrine drew pilgrims from all over Europe.) *seeke* seek

18 *hem hath holpen* helped them *seeke* sick (A saint can intercede with God for sick people who pray to him.)

19 *Bifil* it happened *seson* season

20 *Southwerk* Southwark (Borough across the Thames from the City) *Tabard* Tabard Inn

22 *corage* spirit

25 Of various sorts of people fallen by chance

26 *felaweship* fellowship

27 *wolden* wished to

28 *chambres* bedrooms *wide* spacious

29 And we were made very comfortable in the best way

30 *to reste* setting

32 *hem everichon* every one of them

33 *made forward* (we) made agreement

34 *ther as* as *devyse* shall tell

35 *natheless* nonetheless

36 *Er* before *pace* proceed

37 *Me thynketh it* it seems to me *resoun* proper order

38 *condicioun* state

39 *ech of hem* each one of them

40 And of what occupation and rank they were

41 *eek* also *array* dress

42 *than wol* then will

43 *KNYGHT* knight (professional mounted cavalryman) *worthy* respected

44 *riden out* go on campaign *chivalrie* prowess

46 *Trouthe* integrity *fredom* magnanimity

47 *lordes werre* the war of his feudal superior

48 *ferre* further

49 In Christendom as well as in heathen lands (The Knight has fought on the borders of the Christian West, not against fellow Catholics.)

51 *Alisaundre* Alexandria (Egypt) *wonne* taken (from the Muslims by Peter of Cyprus in 1365)

52 *bord bigonne* sat at the head of the table of honour

53 Above (knights of) all nations in Prussia (whence the Teutonic Knights launched campaigns eastward, against the pagans south of the Baltic, and into Orthodox Russia.)

54 He had ridden on campaign in Lithuania and in Russia. (*Lettow* was not Catholic until after 1386.)

55 *degree* rank

56 In Granada he had been at the siege

57 *Algezir* Algeciras *Belmarye* Benmarin, i.e. Morocco (With the conquest in 1344 of Algezir, their port in Granada, the Belmarin dynasty returned to its Moroccan kingdom of Belmarie, where Christians pursued them.)

58 *Lyeys* Ayash *Satalye* Antalya (Turkish ports taken by Peter of Cyprus)

59 *Grete See* the Mediterranean

60 *armee* military expedition

62 *Tramyssene* Tlemcen (Algeria)

63 *lystes thries* lists three times (in single combat against a Muslim champion) *ay* always

64 *ilke* same

65 *Sometyme* once *Balatye* Balat (Turkey)

66 *Agayn* against

67 And always he had an outstanding reputation

68 *worthy* brave *wys* prudent

69 *port* bearing

70 *vileynye* rudeness

71 *maner wight* kind of person

72 *verray* true *parfit* complete *gentil* noble (All three words have changed in meaning; all are adjectives.)

73 *array* equipment

74 *hors* horses *gay* gaily attired (He cares more for his horses than for his appearance.)

75 *fustian* coarse cotton cloth *gypon* over-tunic

76 *bismotered* marked *habergeon* coat of mail (His tunic is honourably spotted with rust-marks.)

77 *late* recently *viage* expedition

78 *SQUIER* esquire (beginner in knighthood)

79 *lovyere* lover *lusty* zestful *bacheler* bachelor (the first rank of knight)

81 *crull* curly *presse* curler

83 *of evene lengthe* well-proportioned

84 *delyvere* agile

85 *sometyme* for a time *chyvachie* cavalry expedition

86 *Flaundres* Flanders *Artoys, and Pycardie* (parts of France invaded by English armies in the Hundred Years War)

87 *born hym* conducted himself
space space of time

88 *his lady grace* his lady's favour

89 *Embrouded* embroidered
meede meadow

90 *reede* red

91 *floytynge* playing the flute

94 *koude* knew how to

95 *endite* write (words for a song)

96 *Just* joust *purtreye* draw

97 *hoote* passionately
nyghtertale night-time

98 *sleep* slept (The nightingale, which sings all night in the season, is the bird of love.)

99 *lowely* humble
servysable willing to serve

100 *carf* carved (A service of a squire for his knight. To carve for your *fader* was an honour.)

101 *YEMAN* yeoman, free-born servant
he the Knight
namo no more

102 *hym liste* it pleased him

103 *he* the Yeoman

104 *pecok* with flights made from peacock feathers

105 *bar ful thriftily* carried very properly

106 He knew well how to care for his equipment like a true yeoman

107 His arrows did not fall short with limp feathers (The longbow has a range of nearly 300 yards.)

109 *not heed* close-cropped head *broun* dark brown

111 *bracer* arm-guard

112 *bokeler* buckler, shield

113 *gay* bright

114 *Harneised* ornamented

115 *Cristopher* image of saint who protects travellers

116 *bar* bore
bawdryk shoulder strap

117 *forster* forester, gamekeeper *soothly* truly

118 *PRIORESSE* head of a priory of nuns

119 *symple* unaffected
coy shy, reserved

120 *ooth* oath *but* only
Seinte Loi St Eloi (St Eligius, founder of convents, patron saint of goldsmiths.)

121 *cleped* called
Eglentyne Sweetbriar (name from a romance)

122 *soong the service dyvyne* sang the liturgy

123 *Entuned* intoned
ful semely in a most seemly manner

124 *fetisly* gracefully

125 In the manner of Stratford at Bow (where there was a Benedictine convent)

126 *unknowe* unknown

127 *At mete* at table
with alle indeed

128 *leet* allowed

130 *koude* knew how to
kepe take care

131 *fille* fell

132 She took great delight in courtly manners

133 *over* upper

134 *hir coppe* her cup
ferthyng farthing-sized spot

136 *after hir mete she raughte* she reached for her food

137 *sikerly* certainly *greet desport* grand deportment

138 *port* bearing, manner

139 And took pains to represent the manners

140 *estatlich* dignified

141 And to be held worthy of respect (St Benedict's Rule prescribed dignity to a head of house.)

142 *conscience* moral sense

143 *pitous* compassionate

144 *saugh* saw

146 *Of smale houndes* some little dogs

147 *flessh* meat *wastel-breed* fine white bread

148 *soore* bitterly *oon* one

149 *men smoot* someone hit *yerde* stick
smerte smartly

151 Her wimple (head-dress) was pleated in a most proper manner

152 *tretys* well-formed

154 *sikerly* surely
undergrowe not fully grown

155 *spanne* stretch between thumb and little finger
trowe believe

156 *hardily* certainly

157 *Ful fetys* very elegant *was war* noticed

158 *smal* slender

159 *peire of bedes* set of beads, rosary *gauded* decorated (A set of rosary beads with the ten Ave Maria beads separated by more decorative *gauds* for Our Fathers.)

160 *sheene* beautiful

161 *write* engraved
A a capital A (for Queen Anne; also for Amor)

162 *Amor vincit omnia* Love binds (or conquers) all

164 *chapeleyne* assistant *preestes thre* three priests (Too many? One Nun's Priest appears later.)

165 There was a Monk, a surpassingly fine one

166 *outridere* rider-out, supervisor
venerie hunting
(A fat hunting Monk was a favourite butt of satire.)

167 A fine figure of a man, good enough to make an abbot

168 *deyntee* fine

169 *rood* was riding
heere hear

170 *Gynglen* jingle

172 Where this lord was in charge of the house

173 *reule* Rule *Maure* Maurus (who took to France the Rule of St *Beneit*, Benedict of Nursia (*c*480-*c*550), founder of western monasticism.)

174 *somdel streit* somewhat strict

175 *ilke* same *leet* let
pace pass

176 And observed the liberty of modern times

177 He did not give a plucked hen for that text

178 (A comment on such biblical hunters as Esau.)

179 *Ne* nor *reccheleess* heedless (of discipline)

180 *til* to
waterlees out of water

182 *thilke text* that text (a monk vowed to stay in his monastery.)

184 *What* why! *wood* mad

185 *alwey* always
poure pore over

186 *swynken* work

187 *Austyn bit* St Augustine commanded (writing that monks should support themselves by manual work)

188 Let Austin keep his hard work to himself!

189 *prikasour* hunter on horseback *aright* all right

191 *prikyng* tracking

192 *lust* pleasure

193 *seigh* saw
purfiled finely sewn

194 *grys* a fine grey squirrel fur

195 *festne* fasten

196 *of...pyn* a very notable pin fashioned in gold

197 *love-knotte* elaborate device *gretter* bigger

198 *balled* bald
glas glass, or glaze

199 *enoynt* anointed with oil

200 *poynt* physical condition

201 *stepe* prominent *heed* head

202 Which gleamed like the flames under a cauldron

203 *souple* supple, uncreased

205 *forpyned goost* spirit wasted by suffering (the Monk's view of asceticism)

206 *roost* roast meat

207 *palfrey* horse *berye* berry

208 FRERE friar *wantowne* attractive

209 *limitour* friar licensed to beg in a district
solempne impressive

210 *ordres* orders (Franciscans, Dominicans, Carmelites, Augustinians) *kan* knows

211 *muchel* much *daliaunce* sweet-talking

212 *maad* arranged

213 *cost* expense (He paid the dowry.)

214 *post* pillar, support

215 *famulier* intimate

216 With franklins throughout his district. (For the hospitality of franklins, see 331-60.)

217 *eek* also *worthy* prosperous

219 *curat* parish priest

220 *licenciat* licensed to hear confessions

221 *swetely* sweetly

223 *esy* lenient *yeve* give *penaunce* penance, penalty

224 Where he knew he would get a good contribution

225 For to give to a poor order

226 *yshryve* absolved of sin

227 *he yaf* a man gave *he...avaunt* the friar dared assert

228 *wiste* knew *repentaunt* contrite

229 *so...herte* is so hard-hearted

230 He is not able to weep, though he feels very sorry

231 *preyeres* prayers

232 *moote yeve* must give

233 *typet* tippet, tip of the hood *farsed* stuffed

234 *pynnes* pins (see 160 and 196) *wyves* women

235 *murye note* pleasant singing voice

236 *koude* knew how to *rote* stringed instrument

237 In singing ballads he took the prize outright

238 *flour-de-lys* lily

239 *Therto* in addition (Champions were used in judicial ordeal by battle.)

241-2 And every innkeeper and barmaid, better than a leper or a beggar-woman (whom Christians should befriend)

244 It suited not, by virtue of his office

245 *sike* sick

246 *honest* honourable *avaunce* be advantageous

247 *swich poraille* such riff-raff

248 *vitaille* victuals

249 *over al, ther as* in general, wheresoever

250 *lowely* humbly

251 *nas* was not *vertuous* effectual

252a *ferme* payment *graunt* licence (to beg)

252b *haunt* territory

253 *sho* shoe (of no value)

254 'In principio' In the beginning (opening words of St John's Gospel and of the old Latin Mass; a greeting.)

255 *ferthyng* farthing, fourth part of a penny

256 *purchas* takings *rente* cost of the licence

257 *rage* play *right a whelp* just a puppy

258 *lôve-dayes* days for out-of-court settlements (in which the Friar acted as a broker)

259 *cloysterer* cloister-dweller (like a monk)

260 *cope* priest's top-garment

261 *maister* Master of Arts

262 *worstede* woven woollen cloth
semycope short cape

263 That was as round as a bell from the (foundry) mould

264 *lipsed* lisped *for his wantownesse* as a whim

266 *songe* sung

267 *aryght* just

268 *sterres* stars

270 MARCHANT merchant (The first pilgrim from the Third Estate, the workers.)

271 *mottelee* parti-coloured woven cloth *hye* high

272 *Flaundryssh* Flemish *bever* beaver

273 *fetisly* neatly

274 *resons* opinions *solempnely* impressively

275 *Sownynge in* tending to *wynning* profit

276 He wanted the sea to be guarded at any price

277 *Middelburgh* Dutch port *Orewelle* Orwell, nr Ipswich

278 *koude* knew how to *sheeldes* ecus (French coins with a shield on one face)

279 *bisette* employed

280 *wighte* creature

281 *estatly* dignified *governaunce* conduct

282 *bargaynes* lending and borrowing
chevyssaunce dealing

283 *For sothe* truly *with alle* indeed

284 *noot* do not know

285 CLERK university student reading for Holy Orders

286 *unto...ygo* devoted himself to

287 *leene* lean

288 *he* he himself *undertake* promise

289 *holwe* emaciated *therto sobrely* gravely as well

290 *overeste* topmost *courtepy* short cape

291 *geten...benefice* not yet got himself a living

292 *office* secular position

293 *hym was levere* he would rather

294 *clad* bound

295 *Aristotle* The philosopher whose works, translated from Arabic, were the basis of university study from the C12.

296 *fithele* fiddle *sautrie* psaltery

297 *al be* although *philosophre* philosopher/alchemist

298 *cofre* chest (the 'philosopher's stone' of the alchemists turned base metal into gold; but logicians made no money.)

299 *hente* get

301 *bisily gan preye* earnestly did pray

302 *hem* them *scoleye* study in the Oxford Schools

303 *cure* care *heede* notice

304 *Noght o* not one

305 *in forme and reverence* formally and respectfully

306 *quyk* pregnant *hy sentence* elevated content

307 *Sownynge in* tending to

309 *SERGEANT OF THE LAWE* lawyer for the Crown (the highest legal rank) *war* shrewd

310 *Parvys* porch of St Pauls Cathedral (where clients met Sergeants)

313 *swich* so

314 *Justice* judge *assise* court of assizes (where only Sergeants could sit)

315 By open (royal) letter (of appointment from the king) and with full jurisdiction

316 *science* knowledge *renoun* reputation

317 *fees and robes* (a formula) annual payments *oon* a one

318 *purchasour* buyer of land *noon* not one

319 *fee symple* ownership direct from the Crown

320 *been infect* be invalidated

321 *nas* was not

323 *caas* cases *doomes* judgements

324 *William* the Conqueror *were falle* had happened

324 *koude endite* knew how to draft *thyng* contract

325 *pynche* find fault

327-8 And he knew by rote every statute in its entirety. He rode unpretentiously in a parti-coloured coat

329 *ceynt* belt *barres smale* narrow stripes

330 *array* dress

331 *FRANKELEYN* Franklin, country landowner

332 *dayeseye* daisy

333 His temperament was sanguine

334 *morwe* morning *sop* piece of bread (a light breakfast)

335 *delit* delightfulness *wone* custom

336 *owene* own *Epicurus* Athenian philosopher (who held pleasure to be the chief good.)

337 *That* who *pleyn delit* pleasure in itself

338 *verray felicitee parfit* true complete happiness

339 He kept a great household

340 *St Julian* patron of hospitality *contree* part of the world

341 *after oon* of one standard (the best)

342 *envyned* stocked with wine

343 *bake* baked (in a pie) *mete* food

344 *plentevous* plentiful

345 *snewed* snowed

347 *After the sondry* according to the varying

349 *partrich* partridge *muwe* cage

350 *breem* bream *luce* pike *stewe* fish-pond

351 *Wo* unhappy *but if* unless *his* the cook's

352 *Poynaunt* piquant *geere* gear

353 *dormant* standing

355 He presided at sessions of the county court

356 *knight of* M.P. for

357 *anlaas* dagger *gipser* purse

358 *Heeng* hung *morne* morning

359 *shirreve* sheriff *contour* auditor

360 *vavasour* feudal landholder

361 *HABBERDASSHERE* retailer of hats etc.

362 A Weaver, a Dyer and a Tapestry-weaver (As a Carpenter would not belong to a cloth guild, the five Guildsmen must be in a parish guild.)

363 *o lyveree* a single civil uniform

364 *fraternitee* guild

365 *geere* gear *apiked* trimmed

366 *chaped* mounted

370 *yeldehalle* guildhall *deys* dais

372 *shaply* suitable (But no member of these trades became an alderman of London for a century.)

373 *catel* property *rente* income

376 *ycleped* called *madame* title of an alderman's wife

377 And to go in front of everyone else in procession on vigils (of feast days)

378 *roialliche ybore* royally carried

379 *nones* occasion (The Cook is specially hired.)

380 *marybones* marrow-bones

381 *poudre-marchant* spice-powder *tart* sharp

382 *knowe* assess (The Cook is later so drunk that he falls off his horse.)

383 *koude* know how to *sethe* boil

384 *mortreux* stews

385 *thoughte me* seemed to me

386 *shine* shin *mormal* dry ulcer

387 *blankmanger* chicken mousse *with* equal to

388 There was a Ship's Master, dwelling far to the west

389 *woot* know *Dertemouthe* Dartmouth (Devon)

390 *rouncy* carthorse *couthe* knew how

391 *falding* coarse woollen cloth

392 *laas* cord

394 *hewe* hue

396 *ydrawe* transported; also, drawn off, removed

397 From Bordeaux-way while the merchant was asleep (Chaucer's family imported wine from English Gascony.)

398 *nyce* scrupulous *keep* notice

399 *hyer hond* upper hand

400 *hem* them (He drowned his prisoners.)

401 *craft* skill

402 *stremes* currents *hym bisides* near at hand

403-4 His harbourage, lunar position, and navigation, there was no-one like him from Hull to Cartagena

405 *wys to undertake* prudent in undertakings

408 *Gootland* a Baltic island *Finistere* in Galicia, Spain

409 *cryke* creek *Britaigne* Brittany

410 *Maudelayne* (A ship of this name is recorded in Dartmouth, its master in 1391 a Peter Risshenden.)

411 *DOCTOUR OF PHISIK* physician. (Doctoral studies lasted 15 years and more.)

412 *To speke* if we speak

414 *grounded* instructed *astronomye* astrology

415 *kepte* observed

416 *In houres* at the astronomical hours *magyk natureel* science

417 He knew how to find the Ascendent in favourable position

418 *ymages* talismanic figures

420 *were it* whichever of (the four qualities linked to the four elements)

421 *humour* a bodily fluid

422 *verray parfit* true, complete *praktisour* practitioner

423-4 The cause once diagnosed, and the source of his disease, he at once gave the sick man his remedy

426 *letuaries* medical syrups

427 For each of them (doctor and apothecary) made the other to gain

429 *Esculapius* patron divinity of Greek medicine

430 *Deyscorides, Rufus* ancient Greek authorities

431 *Ypocras* Hippocrates, the founder of medicine *Haly* a Persian *Galyen* Galen

432 *Serapion, Razis* Arab writers *Avycen* Avicenna

433 *Averrois* Averroes *Damascien* Arab authority *Constantyn* African translator from Arabic

434 Three recent British authorities

435 *mesurable* moderate

438 Scepticism, an occupational disease of doctors

439 *sangwyn* red *pers* blue

440 *taffata, sendal* silks

441 *but esy of dispense* not quick to spend money

442 He kept what he gained in the plague (The Black Death of 1349, which killed one in three English people, was the worst of four outbreaks of bubonic plague in Chaucer's time.)

443 *cordial* medicine for the heart

445 *WIF...OF biside BATHE* woman from near Bath

446 Except that she was a bit deaf, which was a pity

447 *swich an haunt* such a practice

448 She surpassed those (the weavers) of Ypres and Ghent

450 Who should go up at the Offertory before her

451 *ther dide* any did so *wrooth* angry

452 *charitee* Christian love

453 Her linen head-coverings were very finely woven

454 *dorst swere* dare swear *weyeden* weighed

456 *hosen* stockings

457 *streite yteyd* tightly laced *moyste* supple

460 (The civil marriage took place *at chirche door*) *Fyve* is the number of husbands had by the woman at the well in John's Gospel, Chapter 4.

461 *Withouten* not counting

462 But there is no need to speak of that just now

463 *thries* thrice

464 She had crossed many a foreign river

465 *Boloigne* Boulogne-sur-Mer, a shrine of the Virgin

466-7 In Galicia at Santiago and at Cologne (shrines of James the Apostle and of the Three Kings). She knew a lot about wandering along/off the road

468 *Gat-tothed* with teeth widely set (a sign of Venus)

469 *amblere* ambling horse *esily* comfortably

470 *Ywympled wel* with a large wimple

471 As broad as a buckler or a shield

472 An over-skirt loose about her hips

473 *spores* spurs

474 *carpe* talk

475 Of the cures for lovesickness she knew by chance

476 *the olde daunce* the whole art

477 *povre PERSOUN* poor parson *TOUN* village

482 *parisshens* parishioners

483 *Benygne* gracious

485 And so he was proved to be many times

486 He was very loath to excommunicate for his tithes (Tenth of each income, due to the priest, who had to excommunicate in public those who refused.)

487 *yeven* give *out of doute* in fact

489 *offryng* Offertory *substaunce* stipend

492 *lefte* neglected

493 *meschief* misfortune

494 *ferreste* furthest *much and lite* great and small

498 *tho* those (Matthew 5:17)

501 *foul* corrupt

502 *lewed* untaught, lay

503 *take keep* pay attention

504 *shiten* covered in excrement

507 He did not rent out his living

508 Nor left his sheep stuck in the mire (of sin)

509 *Seinte Poules* St Pauls Cathedral, London

510 To get himself a chantry for souls (singing masses for the soul of a patron)

511 Or to be retained (as chaplain) by a guild

512 *kepte* guarded (John 10:12)

513 *myscarie* come to grief

516 *despitous* contemptuous

517 *daungerous ne digne* disdainful nor haughty

518 *discreet* courteous

521 *But* unless

522 *lough* low

523 *snybben* rebuke *for the nonys* therefore

525 *waited after* looked for

526 *spiced* overscrupulous

529 (The PLOWMAN is a freeman, not a bonded labourer.)

530 Who had pulled many a cart-load of dung

531 *swynkere* worker

533 *hoole* whole (Matthew 22:37-9)

534 *gamed or smerte* pleased or pained

535 And then his neighbour just as himself

536 *dyke and delve* make ditches and dig

537 *wight* creature

538 *hire* payment

540 *propre swynk* own labour *catel* property

541 *tabard* sleeveless tunic *mere* mare

542 *REVE* Steward (The final group is of five dishonest stewards, plus Chaucer.)

543 *SUMNOUR* Summoner (to the church court)

544 *MAUNCIPLE* buyer of provisions

545 *carl* churl *for the nones* all right

547 *proved* was shown *over al* everywhere

548 *ram* ram (the prize)

549 *short-sholdred* thick-necked *knarre* knot in wood

550 *nolde heve of harre* would not heave off hinge

551 *a rennyng* a single run *heed* head